"I DO"

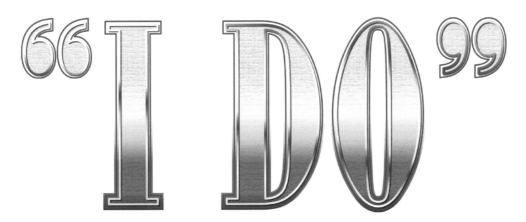

"I DO"

A Christian-Based Alternative to Premarital and Marital Counseling

(Great for couples, pastors, preachers, and therapists)

Joshua DuBoise, BS, MS, LPC

PALMETTO
PUBLISHING
Charleston, SC
www.PalmettoPublishing.com

I Do

First Edition

Hardcover ISBN: 979-8-8229-3328-6
Paperback ISBN: 979-8-8229-2557-1
eBook ISBN: 979-8-8229-2558-8

I Do

A Christian-Based Premarital and Marital Counseling Resource

Great for couples, pastors, preachers, and therapists.

By Joshua DuBoise, MS, LPC

If you're thinking about saying "I do" or you already did, this book is for you.

Contents

Preface

It has been confirmed that couples participating in premarital counseling have a lower divorce rate and increased marital satisfaction. Premarital counseling is an exciting exploration of likes, dislikes, similarities, and differences. It is also a highly useful tool in preparing couples for marriage because it brings to light expectations, reveals insecurities and vulnerabilities, illuminates relationship and conflict patterns, uncovers family-of-origin traditions and baggage, addresses past trauma and its interpersonal consequences, and exposes morals, values, and expected gender roles. This book is not premarital counseling per se; however, it is a self-help resource that addresses subjects and questions like an actual premarital counseling session without an actual therapist to help mediate and explore deeper issues and concerns. Thus, this resource is not a replacement for therapy.

As you brave this path of premarital exploration, abstaining from sexual intercourse is strongly recommended. Sex before marriage can cloud judgment and reason. Having sex during the dating and engagement period can create a smokescreen, preventing both parties from seeing red flags and interpersonal flaws that may later negatively impact the marriage.

Lastly, the content and questions in this resource will likely expose flaws, failures, dysfunction, and a plethora of uncomfortable feelings and memories. Therefore, please be patient with yourself and your partner. When needed, take time away from the material and engage in self-care until you are ready to continue the session. There will be a considerable amount of grace, mercy, kindness, and gentleness needed as you and your partner reflect on the content and answer the questions. Handle each other with care.

Directions

This resource is meant for couples to complete together. It is recommended the couple meet once a week without distractions for roughly an hour to complete each session. Following each session, please fill out the session reflection page if it applies. Please be open and honest with every answer you give—that very important information you're holding back is the very thing your partner needs to know. If a session is lasting longer than one and a half hours, close the session and pick up where you left off the following week. If you and your partner are unable to finish all the sessions or encounter an emotional roadblock, please reach out to a licensed mental health professional.

Philosophy of Marriage

Isaiah 54:5 reads: "For your Maker is your husband—the LORD Almighty is his name—the Holy One of Israel is your Redeemer; he is called the God of all the earth" (NIV).

Marriage is a parable, a type, and a shadow of God's love towards humanity; the depths of God's love are best described in the context of marriage. Why? Because no relationship on Earth is as intimate, sacrificial, long-suffering, or relishing as the marriage relationship. The marriage bond is used to illustrate the gravity of God's devotion to and covenant with Israel and the church. God's love for Israel is unveiled in Hosea 2:19–20, where it is likened unto the marriage bond. It reads, "I will take you to be My wife forever. I will take you to be My wife in righteousness, justice, love, and compassion. I will take you to be My wife in faithfulness, and you will know Yahweh" (HCSB). This scripture testifies to God's desire for His people and His longing for us to know Him deeply.

Furthermore, Paul addresses the church at Corinth, saying, "I am jealous for you with a godly jealousy. I promised you to one husband, to Christ, so that I might present you as a pure virgin to him" (2 Corinthians 11:2 NIV). Again, believers are espoused to Christ, which tells of God's commitment, love, intimacy, and divine relationship with believers. Also see Matthew 2:22; Matthew 25:1; John 3:29; Ephesians 5:25–32; Revelations 19:7–9; Revelations 21:2; and Revelations 21:9 for additional references concerning marriage terminology.

It is no coincidence that Jesus performs His first miracle at a wedding feast (John 2:1–11). Jesus, the Bridegroom of the church, is attending a wedding with His mother and disciples, showing His support and endorsement of marriage. Jesus's presence at the wedding benefited not only the couple but also the couple's friends and family; everyone was positively impacted by the miracle (turning water into wine). It is such an advantage for a husband and wife to invite Jesus into their relationship—especially when it is in need of a miracle! Also, in the beginning of God's love story, God not only created time, space, and everything physical—He also created marriage. Jesus says, "But at the beginning of creation God 'made them male and female.' 'For this reason, a man will leave his father and mother and be united to his wife, and the two will become one flesh.' So they are no longer two, but one flesh" (Mark 10:6–8 NIV). Jesus, reciting Genesis, implies that marriage is neither a cultural construct nor an afterthought of God or humanity, but it is a forethought with divine purpose and intention.

Moreover, God's love story ends with the new heaven and new Earth coming from heaven as a bride adorned for her husband (Revelation 21:2). Revelations 19:6–9 also reveals the great marriage supper that will take place as Christ is eternally united with His bride—the saints—at the Second Coming. Further, Paul writes to the church at Ephesus describing the gender-specific roles of husband and wife as they relate to specific functions of the church in relation to Christ (Ephesians 5:22–31). Moreover, in verse 32, Paul then reveals the great mystery of marriage, explaining that marriage is a parable, a parallel, and a symbolic representation of the intimacy, submissiveness, selflessness, and sacrificial and unconditional love between Christ, the bridegroom, and His church, the bride. What a sobering thought to ponder—marriage, from the beginning of creation, was a symbolic prophecy of the gospel of Jesus Christ; it is the marriage relationship, which every culture around the world possesses, that testifies of Jesus's saving grace and love for imperfect people.

Proverbs 18:22 ESV

"He who finds a wife finds a good thing and obtains favor from the Lord."

In the Beginning, Marriage

The creation of Adam and Eve provides great insights into the differences yet compatibilities of man and woman (husband and wife). Genesis 2:18 says, "The Lord God said, 'It is not good for the man to be alone. I will make a helper suitable for him'" (NIV). The Hebrew word for "suitable" is *neged*, which translates to "in front of," "in sight of," "on the other side of," or "opposite to." Understanding the original language reveals that Eve, who symbolizes all women, is the other side, or the opposite, of Adam, who symbolizes all men. For a visual understanding, it's as if Eve is standing right in front of Adam as a mirror reflecting his opposite. Understanding that both man and woman are made in God's image, we can see women possess qualities likened unto God that Adam does not; similarly, Adam possesses qualities likened unto God that Eve does not. However, together, both Adam (man) and Eve (woman) provide a more accurate understanding of God's nature.

Moreover, Genesis 2:7, which states, "Then the Lord God formed a man from the dust of the ground and breathed into his nostrils the breath of life, and the man became a living being" (NIV), and Genesis 2:22, which states, "Then the Lord God made a woman from the rib he had taken out of the man, and he brought her to the man" (NIV), identify two distinct processes used to create man and woman. The processes that brought about Adam's and Eve's existence are drastically dissimilar; Adam was formed and fashioned from dirt, similar to how a potter molds clay; Eve was made, *banah*, from Adam's rib. The Hebrew word *banah*, which translates to "made," is defined as "built"; this is unlike the process in which Adam was made. The Hebrew word for "built" is used over three hundred times in scripture, and it mostly refers to the design and construction of cities, towers, and altars. In short, man and woman were created as equals but designed in uniquely different ways, which gives a reason as to why the sexes are so different.

God is the creator of all things. He determined it imperative to explicitly identify gender differences in the beginning, for it is written: "So God created mankind in his own image, in the image of God he created them; male and female he created them" (Genesis 1:27 NIV). Therefore, some inherent traits and characteristics solely belong to male or female; this fact is explicitly obvious when surveying the body's design and anatomy. Also, recognizing that Adam was made in the image of God implies there is something about men that reflects God's image. Furthermore, seeing that Eve was made in God's image implies there is something about women that reflects God's nature, too. It must follow that man and woman are both equally necessary beings. When man and woman are joined together in holy matrimony as one flesh, their gender-specific attributes more accurately reflect the image of God.

1 Peter 3:7 ESV

"Likewise, husbands, live with your wives in an understanding way, showing honor to the woman as the weaker vessel, since they are heirs with you of the grace of life, so that your prayers may not be hindered."

Session One

History of the Relationship

Having couples discuss the history of their relationship can provide much insight into their relationship dynamics. When discussing the history of the couple's relationship, one is able to detect areas of disagreement, assess areas of shared meaning, recognize disappointments, evaluate fondness and admiration, learn the uniqueness of each partner, and understand their philosophy concerning the overall relationship. Usually, problems that arise during the dating and engagement period spill over into the marriage—and not only do these problems spill over into the marriage, but they also become even more problematic. Niehuis, Skogrand, and Huston (2006) found that dating patterns foretell the failure of love and affection during the beginning years of marriage. Furthermore, Niehuis et al. (2006) explain: "Feelings of love early in marriage declined for the husbands only when the development of couples' commitment to marry was very turbulent and when the couple experienced frequent conflict in their premarital relationship."

Oral History

Using the Oral History Interview Summary adapted from John and Julie Gottman, questions pertaining to the couple's history and demographics will be explored. This assessment strategy is adopted from the Gottman Method Couples Theory (2016). Take turns answering the following questions and take breaks if needed.

Oral History Inquires

Let's discuss how you met and got together. Do you remember when you met for the first time? Talk about it. Was there anything about your partner that made her/him stand out? What were your first impressions of each other?

1. When you think back to the time you were dating, before you committed to each other, what do you remember? What stands out? How long did you know each other before your commitment? What do you remember of this period? What were some of the highlights? Some of the tensions?

2. Talk about how the two of you decided to commit to each other. Of all the people in the world, what led you to decide that this was the person you wanted to be with? Was it an easy decision? Was it a difficult decision?

3. Looking back over the relationship, what moments stand out as the really good times in your relationship? What were the really happy times? What is a good time for you as a couple? Has this changed over time?

4. Many couples say that their relationship goes through periods of ups and downs. Would you say that this is true of your relationship? Explain.

5. Looking back, what moments stand out as the really hard times in your relationship? Why do you think you stayed together? How did you get through these difficult times? What is your philosophy about how to get through difficult times?

6. Successful relationships take work. Talk about what you think makes a relationship work and what makes it fail.

7. Talk about what you currently know about your partner's major worries, stresses, hopes, and aspirations. How do you stay in touch with one another on a daily basis? What are your routines for staying in emotional contact?

Additional Inquires

1. Briefly talk about why you decided to get married. Have you ever felt this way about a previous partner? If so, why didn't you marry them?

2. What do your friends and family think about your relationship?

3. What have you learned or found interesting about your partner thus far?

Session Reflection

What did you learn about your partner this week?

_____

_____

_____

_____

_____

What did you appreciate about this session?

_____

_____

_____

_____

_____

What is an issue that arose during this session that you would like to discuss at another time?

_____

_____

_____

_____

_____

Additional Notes

_____

_____

_____

_____

_____

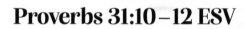

Proverbs 31:10–12 ESV

*"An excellent wife who can find? She is far more precious than jewels.
The heart of her husband trusts in her, and he will have no lack of gain.
She does him good, and not harm, all the days of her life."*

Session Two

Family of Origin

Solomon states, "Train up a child in the way he should go; even when he is old he will not depart from it" (Proverbs 22:6 ESV). What a sobering thought for parents. "Parents are powerful role models," especially when expressing love, affection, and anger (Balswick and Balswick 2014, 74). Fathers teach their daughters how a man is supposed to treat a woman by the way he relates to their mother. He also instructs his son on how to treat his wife as his son observes the way his father relates to his mother. Similarly, mothers explicitly and indirectly send messages to their daughters about how a wife is supposed to interact with her husband by the example she provides when relating to her daughter's father. She also instructs her son through her example, showing him how a wife is supposed to treat her husband through the way she behaves with his father.

Moreover, most of what parents model as a married couple will profoundly influence their children's behavior, opinions, and expectations about marriage as marriage partners. No matter how adamant children are about not behaving like their parents—especially concerning relationship dynamics—when a similar situation arises in their own family, their automatic reaction will be to act similarly to what their parents modeled (Balswick and Balswick 2007). Parents are the interpersonal architects of their child's future. When two people come together in marriage, they are coming as an extension of their families of origin, the family in which they were raised. Regarding one's family of origin—no matter how healthy or dysfunctional it was—it is natural for a person to unconsciously recreate their old family cycles and attachment patterns in their new marriage or family.

Each future spouse's experiences originating in his or her particular family of origin are significant preparations for their marriages and families (Balswick and Balswick 2007). Newlyweds bring to their current relationship conflict styles, communication patterns, morals, values, traditions, gender roles, and peculiar ways of getting their needs met, which mostly stem from their family of origin. Both parties maintained a function—the peacemaker, blamer, scapegoat, victim, caretaker, rebel, surrogate mother or father, or savior—in their family system.

Interestingly, some research suggests that wives are more influenced by their family of origin than their husbands. According to Topham, Larson, and Holman (2005), it is the wife's family of origin encounters that are more powerful than the husband's family of origin encounters when predicting perceived marital hostility. Topham et al. (2005) propose their research "supports other research which suggests that wives are the 'chief architects' of the marital relationship. That is, wives are primarily responsible for the structure and climate of the relationship (Holman & Birch, 2001; Wamboldt & Reiss, 1989)" (115).

During this transition into married life, newlyweds must submit to the pruning process if they want their marriage to last. Regarding landscape and vegetation, pruning is cutting away dead or overgrown branches, stems, or produce, primarily to increase the fruitfulness and growth of each plant, shrub, tree, or flower—the same is true for marriage. Newlyweds must be willing to identify and correct faulty attitudes and beliefs, poor communication patterns, and unhealthy ways of expressing emotions for the marriage to be fruitful. Some traditions will have to die for new family traditions to arise. Some gender roles may have to be reevaluated to increase and sustain martial satisfaction.

Concerning family of origin and marital satisfaction, Balswick and Balswick (2014) state that there are three predictors of marital quality: couples whose parents have had a high-quality marital relationship, couples whose parents have achieved a long-lasting marriage (having never divorced), and couples who parents are free from mental illness. Although these family-of-origin dynamics are ideal, finding two people whose parents meet these qualifications might not be realistic. Furthermore, "each spouse's experience growing up in his or her particular family of origin are major preparations for marriage. Accordingly, marriage involves more than a uniting of two individuals, and it is also a uniting of two extended families" (Balswick and Balswick 2014, 73).

Family of Origin Inquiries:
1. Describe your parents' relationship.
2. What are some positive characteristics of your parents' marriage? What are some negative characteristics of your parents' marriage?
3. In what ways are you similar and different from your parents? How do you suppose these similarities and differences will impact your future marriage?
4. What are some traditions from your family of origin that you would like to bring to your new family? Which traditions would you like to leave behind?
5. If you could label your role in your family of origin, what would it be and why? How do you plan on changing or continuing this role in your new family following the marriage ceremony?

Session Reflection

What did you learn about your partner this week?

_____

_____

_____

_____

_____

What did you appreciate about this session?

_____

_____

_____

_____

_____

What is an issue that arose during this session that you would like to discuss at another time?

_____

_____

_____

_____

_____

Additional Notes

_____

_____

_____

_____

_____

Colossians 3:18–19 ESV

"Wives, submit to your husbands, as is fitting in the Lord. Husbands, love your wives, and do not be harsh with them."

Session Three

Communication and Conflict Management

Communication is the foundation of any and every relationship; communication determines the level of closeness and forms the basis for meaningful interactions among couples. Moreover, problems arise when communication is indirect, dishonest, harsh, and abusive. Communication takes on many forms, ranging from one's tone and rate of speech, gestures, facial expressions, physical proximity, and expression of emotions. It's been said, communication in a relationship is like oxygen to life: without it, the relationship dies. Thoughtless communication can result in broken trust, a lost sense of safety, a breach of marriage vows, and emotional withdrawal. It's been observed that communication and conflict patterns in one's family of origin are often duplicated and repeated when attempting to establish a new family. Many of these behaviors and habits of interaction are subconscious.

What we mean to say and what we actually say are often lost in the transmitting of words. Moreover, what one says can be in opposition to what the receiver hears, which also inhibits effective communication. Furthermore, when one receives information, it's reformatted into what they think they hear as opposed to what has actually been said—this happens when personal interpretation and perception are in play, which sometimes aims to confirm a person's biased opinions and ideas about the sender. Therefore, the receiver ends up hearing a message the sender never intended to relay. For this reason, slowing down a conversation by repeating back to your partner what you heard them say is a great way to confirm that both parties sent and received the intended message.

When communicating wants and needs, demands must be reframed as preferences. An unmet demand will result in much anger, hostility, and resentment. Demands are like commandments: if broken, negative consequences follow. However, having preferences makes room for flexibility and grace. It allows people to make mistakes without suffering harsh punishment.

Example of demands and preferences

Demand: You must compliment me so that I feel good about who I am.

Preference: I would prefer you compliment me, but it's okay if you choose not to; I am responsible about feeling good about who I am.

Demand: You must have dinner ready when I arrive home.

Preference: I prefer for dinner to be prepared when I arrive home, but it's okay if it's not. I am competent and have all the resources to prepare a meal for myself.

The Four Horsemen of the Apocalypse

According to Dr. Gottman, the four most dangerous causes of a dysfunctional relationship are criticism, defensiveness, contempt, and stonewalling; these are known as the "Four Horsemen of the Apocalypse," which essentially are negative ways of communicating (Gurman 2008). If any of these horsemen are present in a relationship, little or no progress will be made. Couples must learn to handle conflict reasonably and constructively if they desire to have well-functioning relationship (Gurman 2008).

The first horseman is criticism. Criticism is attacking your partner's personality and character; it's labeling them instead of focusing on their behavior. The one using criticism is implying their partner is intrinsically inadequate. Criticism may include blaming, name-calling, insulting, and assassinating character (Gottman and Gottman 2017). However, Gottman suggests the remedy for criticism consists of five behaviors: stating how you feel; objectively describing the event or behavior that has triggered these feelings; letting your partner know what you would like for him or her to do moving forward, along with stating any other needs surrounding this current conflict; being polite, using "please "and "thank you"; and supplying plenty of appreciation by choosing to notice what your partner is doing right. One scripture readily reminds us how to prevent an argument from escalating due to criticism. Proverbs 15:1 says, "A gentle answer turns away wrath, but a harsh word stirs up anger" (NIV). Our tone of voice and our attitude, along with the words we choose, can either calm conflict or make it worse.

The second horseman is defensiveness. Defensiveness is an attempt to protect yourself from perceived attacks; moreover, defensiveness usually happens following a partner's criticism. Defensiveness usually escalates conflict because the defensive partner will likely blame the other partner for their behavior instead of taking responsibility for it. Defensiveness usually sounds like counterattacking, "yes, but…-ing," and playing the innocent victim. Defensiveness is minimized when the defensive partner chooses to take some responsibility for his or her part in the conflict, disagreement, or misunderstanding. Gottman and Gottman (2017) state that taking responsibility reduces tension and prevents conflict from escalating by helping your partner feel listened to and understood. In short, taking responsibility for your role in conflict and tension promotes peace. As Paul writes, "If it is possible, as far as it depends on you, live at peace with everyone" (Romans 12:18 NIV).

Furthermore, admitting one's role in the conflict is a type of confession. James writes: "Therefore confess your sins [please note that not all conflict involves sin] to each other and pray for each other so that you may be healed" (James 5:16 NIV). Admitting wrong by taking responsibility fosters physical healing, interpersonal healing, and spiritual healing, especially when coupling it with prayer.

Horseman number three is contempt. Contempt is when one person takes a position of superiority, perfection, or supremacy. A contemptuous person thinks others to be beneath them. Moreover, this type of attitude looks for mistakes, failures, and idiosyncrasies with the motive of making the other person feel small and less than. Contempt comes in the form of sarcasm, name-calling, mockery, hostile humor, and insults. What's most damaging concerning contempt is its effects on the receiver's immune system. Gottman and Gottman (2017) state, "Couples who are contemptuous of each other are more likely to suffer from infectious illness (colds, flu, and so on) than other people" (9).

Proverbs 17:22 states, "A cheerful heart is good medicine, but a crushed spirit dries up the bones" (NIV). Receiving contempt can crush self-esteem and be a catalyst for depression. It mentally and emotionally wounds the receiver, creating invisible injuries and consuming them from the inside out. Ultimately, contempt stems from a heart of evil and wickedness. As Proverbs 18:3 says, "When wickedness comes, so does contempt, and with shame comes reproach" (NIV). Contempt can be avoided by verbally describing feelings using "I feel" statements, expressing unmet needs and wants, showing appreciation and fondness by choosing to focus on what your partner is doing correctly. By doing this, couples are highlighting and emphasizing "whatever is true, whatever is noble, whatever is right, whatever is pure, whatever is lovely, whatever is admirable, whatever is excellent or praiseworthy" (Philippians 4:8 NIV).

Moreover, couples ought not "let any unwholesome talk come out of [their] mouths, but only what is helpful for building others up according to their needs, that it may benefit those who listen" (Ephesians 4:29 NIV). In short, Paul encourages believers to use their words for encouragement and healing, and if we must say something negative, we must learn how to say it positively. He writes, "Let your conversation be always full of grace, seasoned with salt, so that you may know how to answer everyone" (Colossians 4:6 NIV).

Lastly, horseman four—stonewalling. Stonewalling happens when one person becomes so emotionally overwhelmed they mentally and emotionally check out while remaining physically present during the conflict. The one who stonewalls refuses to add anything of real value to the conversation, believing that anything they say will only make matters worse. Therefore, they remain physically present out of respect but are no longer listening, thinking creatively, or adding any real input to the dialogue—essentially withdrawing from the interaction. Stonewalling looks like avoiding eye contact, crossing arms, and withholding verbal communication.

Furthermore, stonewalling is also accompanied by an increased heart rate due to the release of the stress hormones cortisol and adrenaline (Gottman and Gottman 2017). When this emotional flooding occurs, it is paramount the couple take at least a twenty- to thirty-minute break or time-out from their discussion and do something truly relaxing and calming, such as walk, jog, read a book, watch a television show, pray, talk with a friend (about something other than the incident), draw, or listen to a favorite song. After the break, the couple must reconnect; the person who called the time-out is responsible for reengaging with the other person to continue the discussion.

Conflict is unavoidable and a regular part of life. It is not a sign of failure. It can lead to change and growth, and it increases awareness of problems, communication styles, and personality types. Moreover, conflict strengthens relationships, relieves pent-up stress, and exposes values, morals, and beliefs. Also, minor conflict, if adequately addressed, can decrease the frequency and intensity of major disputes. Gottman (1994) states, "Fighting, when it airs grievances and complaints, can be one of the healthiest things a couple can do for their relationship" (15). Moreover, one thing that doesn't seem to change when a couple marries is their conflict—there appears to be an insignificant change in levels of conflict and negative ways of handling conflict following the marriage ceremony. Following the ceremony, many couples often notice an increase in interpersonal conflict.

Gottman and Silver (1994) identify three types of conflict styles: validating, volatile, and avoidant. Validating couples, even in the midst of conflict and disagreement, still consider each other's opinion, validate the other's emotions—which is not the same as agreeing with their emotions—and remain interested in what their partner is saying. They pick their battles carefully and look for areas to negotiate and compromise.

Volatile couples fight hard and play hard; their fights are equally as intense as their making up. Volatile couples are concerned about winning the fight with very little interest in hearing what their partner has to say. These couples express more anger, but they know how to laugh, are passionate, and have a great time together when not engaged in battle. Their marriages are passionate and exciting; however, if they're not careful, their constant fighting and bickering can dissolve the marriage.

The last kind of couple, the avoidant couple, agrees to disagree; furthermore, they resolve issues by evading or minimizing them. With avoidant couples, most conflicts never really get resolved—they do an excellent job taking turns and listening to one another, but rarely do they ever attempt to persuade the other of their point of view. Furthermore, they often avoid issues, minimize problems, and choose to focus on their shared meanings, beliefs, and interests as opposed to their differences and areas of disagreement.

Continuing with Gottman's findings regarding communication and conflict management, Gottman suggest couples use a "gentle start-up" and emphasizes the importance of this technique in building healthier communication patterns. By approaching conversations with kindness and empathy, couples can create a safer and more supportive environment for expressing their thoughts and feelings.

A "gentle start-up" is the concept of initiating a conversation or raising a concern in a calm, nonconfrontational, and respectful manner. It involves expressing one's needs and concerns without criticism or contempt, fostering a more constructive and positive communication style. Below, are two examples of a gentle start-up.

Example 1:

Sarah and Alex have been dating for a few months, and Sarah has noticed that Alex has been spending less time with her lately. Instead of confronting Alex with criticism or anger, Sarah chooses a gentle start-up. She calmly approaches Alex and says, "Hey Alex, I've noticed that we haven't been spending as much time together lately, and now I feel a bit distant. I wanted to talk to you about it and see if we could find a way to reconnect and spend more quality time together. What are your thoughts?"

In this example, Sarah uses a nonconfrontational tone, expresses her concerns without attacking or blaming Alex, and invites open communication to find a solution.

Example 2:

Mark and Lisa have been married for several years, and Mark often forgets to do his share of household chores, which frustrates Lisa. Instead of reacting with contempt or irritation, Lisa decides to approach the issue using a gentle start-up. She waits for a calm moment and says, "Hey, Mark, I wanted to talk about how we share household chores. I've noticed that I've been taking on more of the workload lately, and it's been overwhelming for me. I would appreciate it if we could have a conversation about how we can better distribute the responsibilities and make it more balanced. What do you think?"

In this example, Lisa expresses her concerns about the division of household chores using "I" statements, stays calm, and invites Mark to participate in finding a solution together.

In short, by using a gentle start-up approach, both individuals in these examples create a nonthreatening atmosphere, increasing the chances of productive dialogue and constructive problem-solving in their relationships.

Communication and Conflict Management Inquiries:

1. How was anger expressed in your family of origin?
2. How did your parents or caregivers respond to your negative emotions, such as sadness, fear, or anger?
3. How did your parents handle conflict?
4. How did your parents handle stress?
5. How did your family respond to stress and crisis?
6. What are good conflict management skills you would like to implement in your marriage?
7. How well do you communicate your feelings, needs, wants, and concerns?
8. Discuss some personal conflict management and communication flaws that may negatively affect the marriage.
9. What is your conflict style—validating, volatile, or avoidant?

Session Reflection

What did you learn about your partner this week?

_____

_____

_____

_____

_____

What did you appreciate about this session?

_____

_____

_____

_____

_____

What is an issue that arose during this session that you would like to discuss at another time?

_____

_____

_____

_____

_____

Additional Notes

_____

_____

_____

_____

_____

Ephesians 5:22–28 ESV

"Wives, submit to your own husbands, as to the Lord. For the husband is the head of the wife even as Christ is the head of the church, his body, and is himself its Savior. Now as the church submits to Christ, so also wives should submit in everything to their husbands. Husbands, love your wives, as Christ loved the church and gave himself up for her, that he might sanctify her, having cleansed her by the washing of water with the word, so that he might present the church to himself in splendor, without spot or wrinkle or any such thing, that she might be holy and without blemish. In the same way husbands should love their wives as their own bodies. He who loves his wife loves himself."

Session Four

Role Responsibilities, Headship and Submission, and Intimacy

Role Responsibilities

When deciding to marry, couples bring to their relationship preconceived roles of husband and wife. Often, these roles are a product of their family of origin, society, religion, or a combination of all three. Couples considering marriage must be willing to discuss and negotiate role responsibilities, removing as much ambiguity as possible. Unfortunately, in traditional heterosexual marriages, the majority of parenting and household chores are the wife's responsibility, especially if she is a homemaker—and the same is typically true of the wife who works outside the home.

The following scenario happens all too often. Usually, the husband works eight to ten hours away from home while the wife is also working eight to twelve hours between housekeeping and childrearing. The husband will generally have some degree of quiet time on his drive to work, his lunch break, and on his commute back home, whereas the wife will rarely have a moment of peace and rest when the children are home. Typically, during the evening, the husband walks into the house with the expectation to rest from a hard day's work while the wife continues to parent the children and prepare supper following her husband's arrival. However, when the wife sees her husband walk through the threshold, she thinks to herself, "Finally, my husband is home to assist in parenting the children so that I can take time to rest, relax, and rejuvenate." Please note that husbands providing rest is a Biblical expectation that is often overlooked. Naomi says to Ruth, "May the LORD grant that each of you will find rest in the home of another husband" (Ruth 1:9 NIV).

Additionally, the majority of wives (with children) who are homemakers work between ten to sixteen hours a day, seven days a week—that's seventy to one-hundred and twelve hours!—and many of them have forfeited or postponed their dreams, goals, or careers to answer the call of motherhood. Moreover, wives are unable to have the pleasure of sick days or vacation days. The high demands and expectations placed on wives may be the reason why many women struggle with a decreased sex drive, diminished self-esteem, and a decreased opportunity and motivation to engage in self-care. It is my estimation that many marriages would increase in satisfaction if parenting and household chores were discussed and shared more regularly between husband and wife, whether she is working inside or outside of the home.

Society has now begun the shift in gender role responsibilities, creating a more egalitarian partnership between husband and wife. Fortunately, as a result of this shift in gender roles, Christians now have an opportunity to adopt a more biblically based form of family (Balswick and Balswick 2014).

A biblically based family looks like a woman being praised and esteemed—not on how well her children turn out or how well she manages and maintains the house, but on the basis of her inner beauty and her ability to raise God-fearing children while maintaining a personal degree of piousness and respect for her husband. Moreover, a biblically based family looks like a husband who is open to the influence of his wife; a husband who shares in the burden of household chores and parenting; and a husband who loves his family via serving, sacrificing, and providing emotional support and spiritual leadership. In addition, biblically speaking, husbands are to love and cherish their wives with respect and dignity; to bear principal responsibility for the marriage union and ultimate headship over the family; and to provide food, clothing, and other necessities for their wives (Köstenberger and Jones 2010). Also, research has revealed that a husband who shares domestic duties with his wife has a higher level of marital satisfaction. Several reasons can help explain this phenomenon:

Equality and Fairness: When husbands actively participate in household chores, it sends a message of fairness and equality within the relationship. Shared responsibilities indicate that both partners contribute equally to the family's well-being, creating a sense of balance and mutual respect. This egalitarian approach can contribute to increased satisfaction for both partners.

Reduced Conflict: When couples share domestic duties, it reduces the potential for conflict and resentment related to unequal distribution of household work. This can lead to smoother communication, fewer arguments, and a more positive relationship atmosphere, ultimately enhancing marital satisfaction.

Emotional Connection: Engaging in shared household tasks can provide opportunities for couples to spend quality time together, fostering emotional connection and intimacy. By working together on everyday tasks, couples can strengthen their bond, create shared experiences, and deepen their understanding of each other. This emotional connection contributes to higher levels of marital satisfaction.

Stress Reduction: Domestic duties can be a significant source of stress for individuals, especially when one partner carries the majority of the workload. When husbands actively participate in household chores, the burden is shared, resulting in lower stress levels for both partners. Reduced stress enhances overall relationship satisfaction.

Gender Role Flexibility: Sharing domestic duties challenges traditional gender roles and expectations. Research suggests that couples with more flexible attitudes towards gender roles tend to experience higher marital satisfaction. By rejecting rigid gender norms and embracing shared responsibilities, couples may have healthier relationships and increased satisfaction.

In summary, moving forward in marriage, couples will benefit from open discussions regarding household chores (laundry, washing dishes, feeding and walking the dog, mopping the floors, taking out the trash, etc.), managing and budgeting finances, overseeing car repairs and routine maintenance, and parenting while being careful to not allow the majority of the work to fall to one person. Additionally, the couple must be flexible, allowing for role responsibilities to shift and change, adapting in times of transition (new job, career change, empty nest, a new child or dependent, etc.), and tragedy (misfortune, sickness, or death).

Headship and Submission

Headship and submission are sticky, sensitive topics that have been misinterpreted, misused, and taken entirely out of context—mainly by men—for the purpose of control, abuse, and self-indulgence.

Paul writes in Ephesians 5:22, "Wives, submit to your own husbands, as to the Lord" (HCSB). It is critical to acknowledge that submission is not being oppressed, being made inferior, being cowardly, or being a slave. It is a willful attitude of giving in, putting one's strength under control, or carrying a burden. Submission is the godly calling of a wife to honor and encourage her husband's leadership. Wives are called to submit to their husbands but not because they are exceptional men, not because they are holy, and not because they deserve submission—wives are called to submit to their husbands out of their love toward God. Wives must know that having a sinful or unbelieving husband does not excuse God's command to submit. Peter addresses this fact when he writes, "Likewise, wives, be subject to your own husbands, so that even if some do not obey the word, they may be won without a word by the conduct of their wives, when they see your respectful and pure conduct" (1 Peter 3:1 ESV), which implies a wife's submissive spirit may lead to a believing, faithful, and committed husband. However, wives must know they have independent spiritual intelligence, which means they are not to submit to nor endorse the sins of their husbands.

Continuing, Ephesians 5:23 says, "For the husband is the head of the wife even as Christ is the head of the church, his body, and is himself its Savior" (ESV). It is important to note that headship is not the right to rule, abuse, oppress, or dictate. Headship is the godly calling of a husband to take principal responsibility for Christlike service, leadership, protection, and provision in the home. Moreover, Paul says, "Husbands, love your wives, just as Christ loved the church and gave himself up for her" (Ephesians 5:25 ESV). For husbands to fully understand their responsibility to their wives, they must first understand the character of Christ concerning the church. Christ desires to be one with His bride, calling her His body. He is selfless towards her; He operates with her best interest as the motive for His behavior. He offers grace and mercy in all of her failings. Christ took upon Himself the pain that His bride was to endure. The Christlike love a husband has for his wife is compensated by the divine submission a wife gives to her husband, and the divine submission of the wife towards her husband is compensated by the Christlike love her husband gives to her.

In short, scripture indicates that a wife is to submit to her husband as the church does toward Christ, and the husband is to love his wife as Christ loved the church. The husband will benefit from loving his wife like Christ loves the Church, and the wife will profit from submitting to her husband like the church benefits from submitting to Christ. Headship and submission are intended to serve and meet the needs of both parties.

Further supporting the benefit of marriage, a national study revealed couples with high agreement on spiritual beliefs not only were more happily married but also had many other strengths in their marriages. Some of those strengths include better communication, an increase in conflict resolution, feeling closer to their mate, and higher levels of couple flexibility (Olson et al. 2011). Furthermore, religious beliefs are closely related to making healthy lifestyle choices such as lower consumption of alcoholic beverages, less smoking, an increase of social and spiritual support, strong community relations, and increased hope and optimism (Williams, Edwards, Patterson, and Chamow 2011).

Intimacy

Many think intimacy to be synonymous with sex. It's not! Sex is the climax of intimacy. If sex is the dessert, then intimacy is the three-course meal. Intimacy, also known as affection, prepares the heart for sexual expressions of love. Sex is most exhilarating when coupled with sharing joys, laughter, and vulnerabilities. Johnson and Sanderfer (2016) discuss three types of sexual encounters: sealed off, solace, and synchrony. Sealed-off sex refers to sexual encounters that are emotionally bankrupt; they lack authentic interpersonal connection. Moreover, sex is reduced to physical pleasure, sensations, performance, and orgasms. Sealed-off sex often leaves at least one partner feeling used and objectified (Johnson and Sanderfer 2016).

Solace sex aims to provide reassurance and alleviate attachment fears of rejection and abandonment; the main emotional ingredient for solace sex is anxiety. Solace sex fosters feelings of safety, comfort, and value and reminds the couple that everything is okay. If not put in check, sex becomes the only means to calm attachment fears, making it a one-trick pony that can eventually harm the relationship.

According to Johnson and Sanderfer (2016), synchrony sex is when openness and responsiveness, tender touch, and erotic exploration all join together for total fulfillment and satisfaction. Synchrony sex holds in and maintains the secure emotional attachment that is already present in the relationship. This type of sexual bond fosters a sexual experience that is orgasmic, interpersonally deep, playful, aware, and attuned to the other person's arousal; it is selfless and appreciative. You may be asking yourself—how can my partner and I experience synchrony sex? Though the process can be difficult, the answer is simple: intimacy.

Newlyweds often experience a heightened sense of passion, desire, and romanticism. However, without intentional effort from both parties, those intense feelings will eventually fade; therefore, intimacy must be a priority. Intimacy is likened to small, steady deposits into a couple's emotional bank account that keeps the relationship from going bankrupt.

According to Balswick and Balswick (2014), intimacy is being able to share thoughts, feelings, and needs, which, if done correctly, creates a secure emotional attachment to others. Nevertheless, when there is a lack of intimacy, people will act distrustful, withdrawn, and guarded, which generates much misunderstanding and conflict. Also, withholding verbal and nonverbal expressions of feelings inhibits the development of interpersonal closeness with loved ones.

Intimacy is a mixture of overt and covert behaviors that foster a sense of safety, trust, closeness, fondness, and friendship. Intimate behaviors include, but are not limited to: holding hands; gentle touches on the face, neck, leg, and back; soft kisses (especially on the forehead); writing love notes; making short, thoughtful calls and sending kind text messages; giving massages; going on dates; cuddling; laughing with one another; having inside jokes; participating in shared interests together; giving compliments; sharing feelings; listening and showing interest; purchasing small, inexpensive gifts and treats; going on walks; and praying as a couple.

Gottman and Gottman (2017) suggest additional intimate behaviors that are empirically supported to improve marital satisfaction and maintain momentum for an abiding connection. Gottman recommends at least three daily behaviors: engaging in a six-second kiss when parting from one another, "catch your partner doing something 'right' and say thanks for it" (Gottman and Gottman 2017, 3), and having stress-reducing conversation regularly—these are conversations that discuss external stressors (stressors outside the home and marriage) for a least ten minutes while the listener validates, empathizes, and stands as an ally with their partner against the external stressor.

Role Responsibilities, Headship and Submission, and Intimacy Inquiries:

1. What role did your mother play in your family of origin? What role did your father play?
2. What is a woman's role in a marriage?
3. What is a man's role in a marriage?
4. How will chores and domestic responsibilities be handled?
5. Are there any gender-specific roles you expect from your future spouse?
6. How would you define intimacy? What are intimate behaviors?
7. How do you go about getting your needs for closeness met? In what way might you act out if these needs are not met?
8. How do you imagine your sex life?
9. What is your belief concerning sex?
10. How was sex presented to you as a child?
11. Are there any past sexual encounters that may disrupt sexual expressions in your marriage?
12. What might you do if you were not being sexually fulfilled?

Session Reflection

What did you learn about your partner this week?

_____

_____

_____

_____

_____

What did you appreciate about this session?

_____

_____

_____

_____

_____

What is an issue that arose during this session that you would like to discuss at another time?

_____

_____

_____

_____

_____

Additional Notes

_____

_____

_____

_____

_____

Deuteronomy 6:4–9 ESV

"Hear, O Israel: The Lord our God, the Lord is one. You shall love the Lord your God with all your heart and with all your soul and with all your might. And these words that I command you today shall be on your heart. You shall teach them diligently to your children, and shall talk of them when you sit in your house, and when you walk by the way, and when you lie down, and when you rise. You shall bind them as a sign on your hand, and they shall be as frontlets between your eyes. You shall write them on the doorposts of your house and on your gates."

Session Five

Parenting and Spirituality

Parenting

Too often, once children are born into a marriage, couples soon abandon their covenant with their spouse and reestablish a new covenant with their children. Married couples have to understand their covenant is with their spouse and not their children. In fact, when the marriage is healthy, both husband and wife are better equipped to co-parent effectively. Gottman and Gottman (2007) state: "When we have a baby, there is barely time for friendship, let alone passion and romance" (146). Furthermore, "Parents have to stay friends; otherwise, the forces of passion will dwindle and die" (146). In fact, studies show that many marriages end after children leave home, and this is due to the couple not focusing and investing in the marriage but instead on the children. Often, when adult children leave the nest, the husband and wife feel like distant strangers as they have neglected the relationship for so long.

After having children, it is imperative for couples to work doubly hard to protect their marriage. If parents let them, children can monopolize their time, emotions, and energy, leaving the marriage in critical condition. Olsen, DeFrain, and Skogrand (2011) reference a study that reported that the transition from marriage to parenthood increased couples' stress, increased their number of disputes, and decreased their marital satisfaction.

Parents can model positive behavior or negative behavior—whichever it may be—and the child will more than likely learn to imitate their actions. It is the parents and caregivers who serve as emotional and behavioral models for their children. It is well-known that environments filled with wrath, violence, abuse, and intense, uncontrolled anger will produce similar behavior in children. In accordance with psychodynamic theory, Freud "emphasized the importance of providing a positive emotional environment for the child, who needs to believe that the world is a good safe place and parents can be trusted to be kind and consistent" (Olson 2011, 349). Moreover, the majority of one's happiest memories stem from their childhood—remembering people who love one another, who enjoy each other's company, and who are kind to one another (Olson 2011). It can be concluded that if a child is to have happy memories of home and family life, then it is the responsibility of parents and caregivers to create such an environment for these memories to exist.

Dr. John Gottman's 1997 book, *Raising an Emotionally Intelligent Child*, has great empirical evidence in support of the correlation between marital conflict and child behavior. Gottman states, "Just as a tree is affected by the quality of air, water, and soil in its environment, the emotional health of children is determined by the quality of intimate relationships that surround them. As a parent, your interactions with your child's other parent influence your child's attitudes and achievements, her ability to regulate her emotions, and her capacity for getting along with others" (138). Moreover, Dr. Gottman has arrived at the conclusion that "children raised by parents whose marriages are characterized by criticism, defensiveness, and contempt are much more likely to show antisocial behavior and aggression towards other playmates" (139).

Regarding parenting models, results of research by Dr. John Gottman (1997) have suggested that children whose parents practiced Emotion Coaching—an evidence-based parenting model aimed at increasing emotional intelligence—had better overall health, higher academic scores, better peer relations, fewer behavior problems, and more resiliency towards trauma and life stressors. In addition, Gottman and Gottman (2013) also found that children whose parents followed Emotion Coaching had higher scores in reading and math when IQ was controlled for.

Emotion Coaching Parents

- Recognize emotions as an opportunity for connection.
- Notice and respond to low-intensity emotions, which prevents emotional escalation.
- Encourage the expression of emotions.
- Explore the cause of the emotion.
- Assist the child in figuring out what to do about the emotions they are having.

Spirituality

Concerning spirituality, Deuteronomy 6:5–7 reveals that parents must first have an authentic, committed relationship with God before they can effectively pass their faith onto their children. What is in the heart of parents will spill over into the hearts of their offspring. Children naturally like what their parents like, i.e., sports teams, cars, food, people, clothes, etc. This passage also uncovers the fact that faith, religion, and spirituality are not isolated to a particular place, day, and time. Faith happens via everyday interaction, in the normal hustle and bustle of life. God, religion, and spirituality are talked about and lived out consistently in the home.

Also, concerning God's image and His character, parents have primary influence and responsibility. As children grow and develop their ideas about God, faith, and Christianity, they naturally look to their parents. Parents are largely responsible for what children believe concerning God. Parents who are critical, harsh, and impossible to please unknowingly foster an image of God that is condemning, judgmental, and dissatisfied. Moreover, parents who are emotionally dismissive and nonresponsive foster an image of God who is distant, watching humanity suffer from afar. However, parents who are accepting, unconditionally loving, nurturing, emotionally responsive, empathetic, and who provide their children with responsibilities while also holding them accountable for their behavior create a more accurate image and perception of God.

Parenting and Spirituality Inquiries:

1. Do you want children? If so, how many?

2. How would you describe your parents' parenting style? Would your parenting style be different or similar? Why?

3. What parenting skills do you recognize in your parents that you would like to incorporate into your parenting style?

4. In your opinion, what makes a good parent?

5. What are some of your parenting fears? Where do these fears come from?

6. Who will be primarily responsible for providing the physical and emotional care of your children?

7. What does God expect from you as a parent?

8. Who is responsible for the spiritual development of children: the church, the youth minister, the preacher, or the parents?

9. What are your thoughts on how a child should be disciplined? Do you believe in spanking? If so, under what circumstances?

10. How was faith lived out in your family of origin?

11. How can you foster a more spiritual and God-centered atmosphere in your home?

Session Reflection

What did you learn about your partner this week?

_____
_____
_____
_____
_____

What did you appreciate about this session?

_____
_____
_____
_____
_____

What is an issue that arose during this session that you would like to discuss at another time?

_____
_____
_____
_____
_____

Additional Notes

_____
_____
_____
_____
_____

Malachi 2:14–16 ESV

"Because the Lord was witness between you and the wife of your youth, to whom you have been faithless, though she is your companion and your wife by covenant. Did he not make them one, with a portion of the Spirit in their union? And what was the one God seeking? Godly offspring. So guard yourselves in your spirit, and let none of you be faithless to the wife of your youth. 'For the man who does not love his wife but divorces her,' says the Lord, the God of Israel, 'covers his garment with violence,' says the Lord of hosts. So guard yourselves in your spirit, and do not be faithless."

Session Six

Divorce and Its Ramifications

Unfortunately, divorce is a common social ill that is growing in acceptance and expectancy. Divorce, especially if children are involved, has a far-reaching negative impact on families, friends, and community. Divorce can result in many negative consequences, although there are times when divorce is a necessary course of action to alleviate abuse. According to Gottman and DeClaire (1998), some harmful effects of divorce are the father's diminishing role—financial, proximal, and interpersonal—in the child's life, a decrease in relationship satisfaction between the child and their mother, and an increased vulnerability to outside influences such as peers, media, boyfriends, girlfriends, and adult authority figures. Additional emotional and psychological effects of divorce include depression, anxiety, antisocial behavior, low academic performance, prolonged illness, isolation, delinquency, excessive anger, and substance use.

In addition, in some cases, the partner who did not initiate the divorce will often experience financial hardships and is left to care for and parent the children alone; complete all domestic duties; discipline children; work at least one full-time job (many single parents work two jobs); ensure academic proficiency in children; transport children to all appointments and activities; care for sick children; and is responsible for all finances, just to name a few responsibilities.

Balswick and Balswick (2014, 304–305) identify four stages of divorce: first, the emotional divorce, also known as the erosion of love; second, the actual separation; third, legal issues, economic readjustment, mourning, co-parenting arrangements, identity reconstruction, and emotional functioning; and fourthly, personal recovery. Furthermore, the authors conclude that going through the above four stages are similar to experiencing the amount of grief and bereavement associated with the death of a loved one. The implication is divorce involves multiple losses that feel like death. Following a divorce, the former husband, wife, and any children involved are deeply hurt on multiple levels.

Divorce Inquiries

1. What are some nonnegotiables (criteria for divorce) as a spouse? How do you think you would respond if these boundaries were crossed?

2. Have your parents ever been divorced? If so, what happened? How did the divorce affect you?

3. Have you ever been divorced? If so, what was your role in the divorce? What have you learned about yourself as a result of your divorce? In your previous marriage, what things in your control could you have changed to prevent the divorce from happening? How has your previous divorce affected you?

4. How will you ensure that your marriage will not end in a divorce?

5. What are grounds for divorce? Why? What does the Bible say concerning divorce?

6. How are children impacted by divorce?

7. What, in your opinion, prevents divorce?

Session Reflection

What did you learn about your partner this week?

_____

_____

_____

_____

_____

What did you appreciate about this session?

_____

_____

_____

_____

_____

What is an issue that arose during this session that you would like to discuss at another time?

_____

_____

_____

_____

_____

Additional Notes

_____

_____

_____

_____

_____

1 Timothy 6:6 – 10 ESV

"But godliness with contentment is great gain, for we brought nothing into the world, and we cannot take anything out of the world. But if we have food and clothing, with these we will be content. But those who desire to be rich fall into temptation, into a snare, into many senseless and harmful desires that plunge people into ruin and destruction. For the love of money is a root of all kinds of evils. It is through this craving that some have wandered away from the faith and pierced themselves with many pangs."

Session Seven

Money and Marriage

Money and marriage is a topic that demands a significant amount of attention. There is an understandable amount of fear and anxiety when engaged couples and newlyweds consider the subject of finances. Unfortunately, many conflicts, arguments, and disagreements will center around finances. Let's suppose that finances are not discussed regularly, and proper expectations and roles are not fully disclosed. In that case, it can result in mountains of debt, financial crises, loss of investments, depleted retirement funds, repossessions, foreclosures, poverty, damaged credit, and even divorce. On the other hand, when money is managed correctly, discussed openly, and budgeted accordingly, couples can expect fewer conflicts, experience financial freedom, save money, and decrease the overall stress related to economic issues.

As couples transition from "me" to "we," their beliefs, philosophies, and handling of finances must be restructured. What each person does with their money affects the entire household. Therefore, the couple should be joint decision-makers regarding money management. Joint decision-making is ideal because if one partner mismanages money secretly, resulting in financial distress, a barrier of insecurity is often the result. Usually, one person is tempted to keep their loved one out of the financial communication loop due to pride and an attempt to protect the other person from fear, worry, and anxiety. However, once the financial issues become unmanageable and the other partner is informed of the economic hardship, they feel betrayed and deceived.

When conflict surrounding money arises, it is seldom about money and more about the meaning of money. Beneath the surface of money is a more vulnerable and more profound significance. Money is a symbol that represents deeper issues related to trust, safety, security, approval, success, value, control, self-worth, dependence, independence, and a sense of entitlement. Much of a person's beliefs about money can be traced back to their childhood and parents' spending habits.

Financial Inquires

1. How was money used in your family of origin?
2. Who balanced the bank accounts?
3. Who was the primary financial provider in your family of origin?
4. In your family of origin, what messages (implicit or explicit) did you receive concerning money?
5. Are you a saver or a spender?
6. Do you underindulge or overindulge regarding your wants?
7. How much do you earn?
8. What is the balance in your bank account?
9. What is your credit score?
10. How much debt have you accumulated?
11. What improvements do you need to make regarding your spending habits?
12. How much money is enough?
13. How much money do you need to save so that you feel a sense of financial security?
14. How do you feel about separate and joint bank accounts?
15. Which bills do you expect to pay?
16. What if you lose your job or become disabled? How will you make ends meet?
17. What kind of lifestyle do you imagine living?
18. What does money symbolize to you?

Session Reflection

What did you learn about your partner this week?

_____

_____

_____

_____

_____

What did you appreciate about this session?

_____

_____

_____

_____

_____

What is an issue that arose during this session that you would like to discuss at another time?

_____

_____

_____

_____

_____

Additional Notes

_____

_____

_____

_____

_____

1 Corinthians 13:4–7 ESV

"Love is patient and kind; love does not envy or boast; it is not arrogant or rude. It does not insist on its own way; it is not irritable or resentful; it does not rejoice at wrongdoing, but rejoices with the truth. Love bears all things, believes all things, hopes all things, endures all things."

Session Eight

Keeping Marital Satisfaction High

Every couple desires a strong, happy marriage; below are a few suggestions to cultivate such a relationship. Gottman suggests that couples who illustrate strong marriages have gentle start-ups, are accepting of their partner's influence, and are willing to compromise. A gentle start-up can be described as having a calm tone of voice, a soft facial expression, and a mild choice of words. Moreover, it's bringing up conflicts, disappointments, and upsets without blaming, shaming, and criticizing.

Accepting influence means merely being open to the other person's ideas and trusting their partner's suggestions, along with being open to trying things their partner's way as opposed to being confined to doing things one absolute way.

Compromise is the ability to negotiate by fostering a give-and-take relationship. Compromise happens when both partners get a little of what they are asking for; the goal is for the couple to end the discussion satisfied with the agreed-upon concessions.

Also, Dr. John Gottman's research revealed that great marriages maintain a 5:1 ratio—that's five positive interactions to every one negative interaction. It's not that couples meticulously calculate their positive and negative interaction; instead, they have learned to naturally give their partner the benefit of the doubt, they see their partner in a favorable light, they validate their partner's emotions, and they give their partner compliments daily. These all easily counteract and buffer against times of negativity.

Wise Counsel

1. Learn how to down regulate your negative emotions during conflict by calming down and taking breaks.
2. Keep praise and admiration in your daily vocabulary—catch your partner doing something right and acknowledge it.
3. Consider what the other spouse is going through and seek to understand their stressors.
4. Acknowledge your spouse's emotional talk and expressions—this is called validation—before problem-solving.
5. Pick your battles—some issues are not worth fighting over.
6. Schedule important discussions so they can get the time and attention they deserve.
7. Fight in a way that honors and protects your friendship because your friendship determines your level of intimacy and relationship satisfaction.

8. Apologize and forgive often.

9. Don't use or refuse sex in an unfair way; sex should be enjoyed by both parties. Don't use sex as a means of vengeance or manipulation, and talk about your sex life monthly.

10. Don't focus solely on self-satisfaction; focus on pleasing your spouse.

11. Spend time together participating in something you both enjoy.

12. Make date nights a priority, engaging in them at least twice a month.

13. Have healthy outside relationships that benefit and support the marriage.

14. Pray together weekly.

15. Some problems are perpetual, meaning they are ongoing and unsolvable. Though you may not be able to solve the perpetual problems, you can create time and space to talk about them as they arise so that both parties feel heard, valued, and important.

16. When you say "I do," you are stating that you accept your spouse just as they are—the good, the bad, and the ugly. You are implicitly stating nothing about them needs to change. So ask yourself, "Am I willing to live with this person for the rest of my life, just as they are, not wishing they were someone else?" In other words, don't marry a person based on their potential; marry them because you love them for who they actually are.

17. Marriage should not be based on what you can get, but rather what you have to offer.

18. Listen more than you lecture.

19. Have fun!

20. Laugh!

What would you like to add to this list?

1. _____
   _____

2. _____
   _____

3. _____
   _____

4. _____
   _____

5. _____
   _____

Special Interest

Blended Families, Covenant vs Contract, Pornography, Physical Attraction, Trust, Infidelity, and Cohabitation

Blended Families

Blended families face an insurmountable amount of difficulties from which traditional families are exempt. Concerning blended families, there is a great deal of transitioning and adjusting that is inevitable. Family birth order roles may become distorted as a child from the previous family may have been the youngest but now occupies the position of the middle or eldest. A mother who was once single and very close with her child now has to set boundaries with the child to establish a bond with her husband. A husband who was previously married with no children suddenly has to learn how to be a parent figure to a child who did not ask for a stepfather. Other transitions and adjustments include establishing new morning and bedtime routines; deciding on chores and other domestic responsibilities; figuring out new parenting styles; sharing bedrooms and other common areas; and the uncomfortableness of living with a stranger.

Unfortunately, the probability of conflict within blended families is doubly high. If children are involved, opportunities for conflict arise when one spouse appears to display an increased loyalty to biological children as opposed to their newlywed spouse—or the spouse's biological children may feel their parent is more loyal to their new spouse as opposed to their children. Moreover, jealousy may arise between both the stepparent and biological children as they require and expect a considerable amount of attention from their spouse and natural parent. Additionally, because being a blended family also involves blending beliefs about parenting, issues concerning parenting may be the first crisis in a new blended family (Williams et al. 2011).

When deciding to blend a family, great consideration should be given to the previous failed relationship if death was not the reason. It is paramount that the person preparing to enter a blended family first assess both their role and the reason for the dissolution of the previous relationship. If not, the issues from the past relationship will likely manifest in the subsequent relationship. Taking responsibility for personal flaws, mistakes, and failures acted out in the past relationship will help prevent these same issues from being present in the next one. Therefore, a great deal of honesty, self-actualization, and repentance is necessary before moving forward in a blended family.

When children are involved, blending a family requires much preparation. Essential conversation topics must include the disciplining of children (which initially should come from the biological parent until trust and commitment is established), how each child envisions the role of the new stepparent, and how the stepparent envisions their new role. Also, conversations should include what old and new traditions to incorporate into the new family, including how birthdays and holidays will be celebrated, and appropriate boundaries concerning touch, mainly with children. Ultimately, an ongoing goal of blended families should be to decrease interpersonal ambiguity. Interpersonal ambiguity refers to the uncertainty and lack of clarity that can arise when two families come together to form a blended family. It involves confusion and complexity in interpersonal dynamics, where family members are unsure about their roles, expectations, boundaries, and relationships within the new family structure.

Interpersonal ambiguity can manifest in various ways, such as role ambiguity, where family members are uncertain about their responsibilities and positions within the blended family. There can also be uncertainty regarding boundaries, expectations, and the merging of different sets of rules and routines. Loyalties and alliances may be tested as individuals navigate their connections and allegiances between their original family unit and the newly blended family. Identity and belonging can also become ambiguous for children or teenagers in blended families.

To address interpersonal ambiguity in blending families, open communication, empathy, and patience are key. Having honest and ongoing conversations to clarify roles, establish boundaries, and set realistic expectations is important. Seeking professional guidance through family counseling or therapy can also be beneficial in navigating these complexities and building stronger bonds within the blended family.

Overall, understanding and addressing interpersonal ambiguity can help create a more harmonious and connected blended family environment.

In summary, blending a family requires open communication, empathy, and patience. It is essential for blended families to engage in honest and ongoing conversations to clarify roles, establish boundaries, and set realistic expectations. Seeking professional guidance, such as family counseling or therapy, can be beneficial in navigating these complexities and building stronger bonds within the blended family unit.

Covenant vs Contract

"Rather than being merely a contract that is made for a limited period of time, conditional upon the continued performance of contractual obligations by the other partner, and entered into primarily or even exclusively for one's own benefit, marriage is a sacred bond that is characterized by permanence, sacredness, intimacy, mutuality, and exclusiveness" (Kostenbeger and Jones 2010, 78).

In the realm of marriage, there is a stark contrast between theory and practice. While many couples enter into a covenant, their actions and behaviors lean towards a contractual mindset. But what if this gap could be bridged and couples could truly embrace the essence of a covenant relationship? Imagine a marriage that transcends the limitations of a mere contract, one that is built upon the principles of permanence, sacredness, intimacy, mutuality, and exclusiveness. This is the soul of a covenant, a bond that goes beyond the conditional expectations of a contract.

Contracts are often rooted in selfish motivations and predetermined conditions. "If you do this, then I will do that" becomes the mantra of such agreements. They are time-bound, focusing on specific actions rather than nurturing a deep connection. Breach the terms, and repercussions loom, leading to punishment, abuse, or even abandonment. But a covenant breathes new life into the marital union. It is a commitment that knows no end, an unwavering promise to fulfill and bless one another unconditionally. In a covenant, the focus shifts from personal gain to the well-being of both partners and the relationship itself. Forgiveness replaces penalties, compromise paves the way for understanding, selflessness blossoms, and grace embraces every step taken together. In this sacred space, a couple finds solace in the shared journey, knowing that their love is rooted in something far more profound than a mere contract.

At the heart of understanding the essence of a covenant relationship in marriage lies the recognition that God Himself is in a covenant with believers. This profound truth illuminates the sacredness of the marital union and sets it apart from a mere contractual arrangement. As God's covenant with believers serves as a guiding principle, we can draw parallels to the covenant relationship in marriage. Just as God extends His unwavering commitment, love, and grace to His people, so too should couples embrace these qualities within their own marital covenant. By recognizing that marriage is not solely a human construct but a reflection of God's own covenant, couples can gain a deeper appreciation for its significance. It becomes a divine union, where two individuals come together under the sanctity of God's love and guidance. With this understanding, the covenant nature of marriage takes on added meaning. It becomes a testament to the faithfulness, sacrificial love, and unconditional acceptance that God exemplifies in His covenant with believers. Such a realization fosters an environment of spiritual growth, mutual support, and shared purpose within the marital bond.

In short, couples ought to aspire to create a covenant relationship in their marriages, acknowledging and embracing the presence of God within their sacred union. By seeking His guidance and modeling their love and commitment after His, couples can wholeheartedly embrace the covenant nature of marriage, walking hand in hand with their spouse on a remarkable journey of faith, love, and fulfillment.

Pornography

Pornography is a vice that can create an addictive behavior that can destroy relationships. What makes pornography so addictive? There are several factors. One: it is virtually free and therefore cost-efficient. Two: it is literally at one's fingertips; consequently, it is always in close proximity with no travel required. Three: the supply is always on par with the demand; the quantity never runs out. Four: it is not a chemical nor a substance; therefore, it is essentially undetectable. Lastly, the images are carved into the heart of the onlookers, making detox impossible. For all the aforementioned reasons, pornography is a drug like no other.

Pornography is a supernatural stimulant. Pornography takes the natural, innate desire of sex drive and recreates a hypersexual experience that desensitizes its victims to natural and healthy sexual practices over time. When this happens, the natural sex drive is no longer stimulated until a more supernatural sexual stimulant is introduced. Sadly, the onlooker of pornography must gradually turn to more extreme, risky, and sinister means for sexual stimulation, which have grave consequences for marriages and families. Porn addicts (who are mostly male) have reported lower self-esteem, increased anger and aggression towards women, superficiality towards women, a lost sense of connection to others and reality, and depression. Also, those who engage in pornography report making unfair comparisons between their partner or spouse and the pornographic actor or actress. They also report demanding more sex from their partner or spouse, along with an increase in sexually risky behavior such as infidelity, swinging, and ménage à trois. Wives have reported low self-esteem, feeling they will never measure up to the appearance and sexual activity of pornographic actors and actresses. Pornography portrays men, women, and children as objects to be used to satisfy one's sexual pleasures and fantasies. It dehumanizes humanity, reducing people to emotionless, valueless, disposable gadgets who are void of soul, human rights, respect, and dignity.

In conclusion, it is essential to acknowledge that the impact of pornography on marriages is multifaceted and can vary depending on individual circumstances. However, the existing literature consistently identifies negative implications, emphasizing the potential for erosion of trust, distorted perceptions of sexuality, decreased relational satisfaction, an increased risk of infidelity, and adverse emotional and psychological outcomes. Overall, the evidence suggests that pornography consumption within a marital relationship can have detrimental effects on the emotional, sexual, and overall relational dynamics.

Physical Attraction

God has graciously given humanity the gift of relationships. For humanity to reach out for intimate connections with others, He has placed within us an attraction for one another—more specifically, the attraction between a man and a woman. It is the pull of attraction that catalyzes humans to reach out for interpersonal connection with others.

Physical attraction is important in a marriage for several reasons. It enhances intimacy between partners, fostering a sense of desire and closeness. It contributes to a fulfilling sexual relationship, bringing enjoyment and satisfaction. Physical attraction also sustains long-term interest and connection, serving as a catalyst for continued bonding and admiration.

Additionally, feeling physically attractive to one's spouse boosts self-esteem and confidence, which positively impacts overall well-being. Appreciating a spouse's physical appearance creates a sense of delight and appreciation within the marriage.

However, it's important to note that physical attraction is just one aspect of a healthy and balanced marriage, and emotional connection, effective communication, and mutual respect are equally important for relationship satisfaction. From a biblical perspective, physical attraction between men and women is acknowledged as a natural aspect of human relationships, particularly within the context of marriage. The creation account in Genesis highlights the complementary nature of male and female, emphasizing the intimate union between a man and a woman. The book of Song of Solomon celebrates physical attraction and romantic love within the marital relationship.

However, while physical attraction is celebrated within marriage, the Bible also emphasizes the importance of purity and self-control outside of this context. Believers are urged to guard their hearts and maintain sexual purity. The Bible encourages individuals to focus not only on physical attraction but also on character, integrity, and inner beauty. This highlights the significance of qualities such as reverence for God over mere physical appearance.

In Western culture, there seems to be an unhealthy obsession with outer beauty and attraction. Physical attraction appears to supersede less apparent traits when choosing a mate. Outer beauty can mistakenly be labeled as "love," mainly love at first sight. When a person is physically attracted to another, the brain gets flooded with neurochemicals that create feelings of pleasure and euphoria; these feelings and chemicals can last from three months to six years (Olson, DeFrain, and Skogrand 2014). Relationships founded on physical attractiveness can provide a false sense of intimacy, companionship, and connection. Research suggests that chemicals released at the sight of physical attractiveness can inhibit one's ability to think rationally and objectively due to the intense feelings of joy, energy, sociability, and excitement; the release of these feel-good chemicals causes couples to idealize their partner, seeing only their partner's positive traits and overlooking their flaws (Olson et al. 2014). One incredible misunderstanding that researchers have discovered is that people often associate physical attractiveness with other desirable traits, believing that whatever is beautiful is also good and pleasing (Warren 2018). In short, physical attraction is highly esteemed but likely the most superficial characteristic when deciding on long-term commitments.

Trust

Trust is the foundation of any relationship. For a relationship to thrive, trust must be built, fostered, maintained, and nurtured. Glass (2003) asserts that basic trust is developed during childhood, and for individuals who did not develop this basic sense of trust, they are "especially vulnerable to deception by a loved one" (98). When a person feels they are unable to trust their partner to meet their needs, they will likely seek out other relationships to selfishly have their needs and wants satisfied, which can be detrimental to an intimate relationship. When one partner is unable to trust their partner to meet their needs, seeking fulfillment outside of the relationship can be a challenging and delicate situation. It is important to distinguish between healthy and unhealthy ways of meeting one's needs outside of the relationship.

Healthy ways of seeking fulfillment outside the relationship may include engaging in individual hobbies, pursuing personal interests, and forming strong relationships within a supportive network of friends or family. By investing in personal development, seeking emotional support from trusted individuals, and focusing on self-care, individuals can find fulfillment and growth without undermining the foundations of their relationship. These healthy approaches allow for personal growth and strengthen the individual, which can positively impact the relationship as a whole.

On the other hand, unhealthy ways of seeking fulfillment outside the relationship often involve crossing boundaries and engaging in deceit or infidelity. This may include seeking emotional or physical connections with others without the knowledge or consent of the partner. Engaging in secretive behavior, betraying trust, and resorting to infidelity can further damage the foundation of the relationship and hinder the possibility of rebuilding trust and addressing needs within the partnership. The ability to trust one's partner is a great protective factor against infidelity. Below are a few insights on trust that are empirically and spiritually supported.

Trust is increased when a couple's interaction, positive or negative, benefits each of them; Gottman and Gottman (2018) call this "couple payoff." Moreover, they state "trust exists when the behavior exchanges that are most likely in the system are those that maximize the sum of both people's payoffs. Each partner has their partner's back" (Gottman and Gottman 2018, 25). In other words, when one partner behaves in ways to maximize their wants, needs, and desires with little or no regard for the other person, trust is never established or trust is eroded. When trust is correctly established, it creates a homeostatic balance where positive affect prevails over negative affect. Additionally, when trust is low, the couple will create an environment of increased negativity; likewise, when trust is high, the couple will foster an environment of increased positivity.

It is crucial to prioritize open and honest communication within the existing relationship and seek professional guidance if needed to address the underlying trust issues. By fostering trust, engaging in personal growth, and seeking support through healthy channels, individuals can work towards meeting their needs while also maintaining the integrity and well-being of the relationship.

In short, a couple who measures high on trust says, "I will act in ways that are most beneficial for us." How refreshing are Paul's words to the Philippian church: "Do nothing out of selfish ambition or vain conceit. Rather, in humility value others above yourselves, not looking to your own interests but each of you to the interests of the others" (Philippians 2:3–4 NIV). I find it absolutely astounding how God's divine Word, if lived out, is the perfect resource for preventing an affair.

Infidelity

Infidelity in a marriage has the potential to deeply impact and disrupt the cognitive and emotional well-being of both partners involved. The betrayal of trust and the breach of the sacred bond within the relationship can cause profound trauma that reverberates through every aspect of the affected individual's life.

Following an affair, the betrayed partner often exhibits cognitive disruption, emotional turmoil, and behavioral difficulties—determining which response is more damaging is difficult. Besides, according to the American Association for Marriage and Family Therapy (Glass 1999), "The reactions of the betrayed spouse resembles the post-traumatic stress symptoms of the victims of catastrophic events." Also, Olson, DeFrain, and Skogrand (2014) add that the impact of adultery can be as severe as the revelation of sexual abuse (184).

After the discovery of an affair, cognitive disruption is expected. The betrayed partner will often engage in obsessing over the affair until they have all the answers. They will obsess over lies and unanswered questions in their heads. They will regularly fixate on images, fantasies, and puzzling memories that don't quite add up. The betrayed will also often loop the details of the affair over and over again in their mind. Furthermore, cognitive disruptions also include the betrayed partner obsessively visualizing their partner having sex with the other person (Glass and Staeheli 2003), which is often re-traumatizing.

Additionally, the discovery or disclosure of infidelity can shatter long-held beliefs and assumptions about the strength and integrity of the marriage. It introduces doubt, insecurity, and a questioning of one's own worth and desirability. The betrayed partner may struggle to make sense of the situation and seek answers to questions that seem unanswerable. This cognitive dissonance can lead to confusion, a loss of focus, and difficulty in making decisions or trusting one's own judgment.

Concerning the emotional response to infidelity, there is much literature and attention given to the emotional effects of an affair—the emotional forces appear to last months or even years following the affair. Therefore, the emotional response to infidelity appears to be the most damaging. Dr. Shirley Glass has done tremendous, exhaustive work unveiling the emotional effects of unfaithfulness. Dr. Glass states, "In the first minutes and hours after the revelations of infidelity, emotions are out of control" (Glass and Staeheli 2003, 88). Moreover, Glass et al. (2003) indicated that anxiousness leading to panic, along with bouts of clinical depression, manifest in the betrayed partner.

Furthermore, common emotional responses to infidelity include irritability, aggression, and numbing, which occurs when the betrayed partner becomes emotionally numb for a time as a way of psychological protection from pain too difficult to bear (Glass and Staeheli 2003). Surprisingly, some individuals respond with changing emotions—one moment they may be initiating sex and the next moment demanding the betrayer to leave the house and never return.

Grief is also a natural emotional response to infidelity. The betrayed partner has much to grieve as many losses have become a reality. There is a loss of perceived innocence in the betrayer; there is a loss of security, trust, and commitment; a loss of plans and dreams; there is a loss of physical intimacy and emotional connection; and for many, a loss of a relationship, anniversaries, friendships, finances, and assets.

Rebuilding trust after infidelity is a challenging and time-consuming process. It requires genuine remorse, open communication, and a commitment from both partners to actively work on repairing the damage done. Trust is fragile, and its restoration cannot be rushed. It may take years of consistent effort, transparency, and the demonstration of changed behavior to rebuild trust in the marriage. The healing process often involves both individual and couples therapy, providing a safe space for healing, understanding, and rebuilding the emotional bonds. It requires addressing the underlying issues (usually on both sides) that led to the infidelity, fostering empathy and forgiveness, and working towards establishing new patterns of communication, emotional intimacy, and shared values.

It is important to acknowledge that repairing trust does not guarantee the complete restoration of the relationship to its pre-infidelity state. The scars of infidelity may always remain, and the process of healing varies from person to person. Rebuilding trust requires patience, resilience, and a willingness to acknowledge and address the pain and trauma caused by the infidelity.

Overall, infidelity can have a devastating impact on a marriage, causing cognitive and emotional trauma that takes time and concerted effort to heal. Rebuilding trust is a fragile and complex journey that requires commitment, understanding, and a shared desire to salvage the relationship.

Cohabitation

The reality is cohabitation has become the norm and is more popular than ever for Americans (Olson et al. 2014); cohabitation precedes the majority of all marriages. Those advocating for cohabitation assert that couples can experience the realities of life before getting married and it can be a testing ground for marriage—couples can break up and try again with another person as many times as they like without the baggage and woes of divorce. Also, they believe dependent, insecure attached couples can satisfy their needs for connection while learning their partner's habits and triggers before deciding to marry. However, researchers suggest that living together before marriage increases a couple's chance of divorce unless the couple has agreed to marry, set a date publicly, and are engaged; multiple cohabitations is a predictor of future failings of relationships (Balswick and Balswick 2014).

According to Balswick and Balswick (2014), when cohabitating, the idea of commitment is ambiguous. Balswick and Balswick (2014) further revealed that research has found that when they eventually marry, men who cohabitate with women are not as committed to them as compared with men who did not cohabitate with their mate prior to marriage. Moreover, women tend to perceive cohabitation as a step leading to marriage, whereas men tend to view cohabitation as a step leading to commitment (Balswick and Balswick 2014) but not necessarily marriage. This reveals two opposing motives for living together prior to marriage. Furthermore, some even see cohabitation as an alternative to marriage. Other research has found that while cohabitating couples have high levels of commitment, they have low levels of satisfaction, increased negative communication, and more increased physical aggression than non-cohabitating dating couples (Balswick and Balswick 2014).

Additionally, cohabitants, when compared to married persons, had poorer relationships with parents and expressed lower levels of commitment and happiness. Though cohabitation before marriage results in perceived commitment, cohabitation actually correlated with lower commitment levels, increased divorce, lower marital satisfaction, and increased wife infidelity after the marriage ceremony. Additionally, cohabitating couples are less likely to reconcile following a separation when compared to married couples (Balswick and Balswick 2014). In addition, at least in European societies, cohabitation is related to marital instability (Balswick and Balswick 2014).

Another study revealed that married couples who cohabitated before marriage had lower levels of marital interaction (spending time together, eating meals together, shopping together, visiting friends, recreational activities), had more frequent and intense marital disagreement (which included slapping, hitting, punching, kicking, and throwing things), presented with increased marital instability (considering divorce, talking to friends about divorce, seeking legal counsel concerning divorce), and increased frequencies of divorce (Balswick and Balswick 2014).

Further, studies show that children are worse off in cohabitating relationships; cohabitating couples tend to have much higher levels of breaking up, which devastates children. Higher levels of abuse and sexual violence against children are reported among cohabitating couples, and research has exposed that cohabitating couples invest more in their personal welfare than that of the children (Balswick and Balswick 2014).

In conclusion, cohabitation before marriage can present various dangers and challenges to the stability and long-term success of a relationship. It is associated with higher rates of divorce, increased risk of domestic violence, lower relationship satisfaction, and a lack of commitment compared to couples who choose not to cohabitate before marriage. Additionally, cohabitation can mask incompatible or unresolved issues, create a sense of false security, and hinder the development of vital communication and conflict resolution skills. It is crucial for individuals considering cohabitation to carefully weigh these risks and consider alternative approaches to building a strong and healthy foundation for their future marriage.

Thank You!

Dear Readers and Participants,
I want to express my deepest gratitude and appreciation to all of you who have taken the time and put in the effort to complete my book on marriage and premarriage counseling. Your dedication to personal growth and your commitment to building strong and thriving relationships is truly commendable.

Writing this self-help resource has been a labor of love, and I am honored and humbled that you have chosen to engage with its content. Your investment in your own well-being and the future of your relationships is a testament to your wisdom and desire for a fulfilling and harmonious marriage.

I sincerely hope that this book has provided you with valuable insights, practical tools, and thought-provoking guidance. My ultimate wish is that the knowledge you have gained from this resource empowers you to navigate the complexities of marriage with confidence, compassion, and resilience.

Thank you for trusting me as your guide on this journey. Your commitment to personal growth and your enthusiasm for creating fulfilling relationships inspire me. May this resource serve as a foundation for a beautiful and meaningful marriage.

With heartfelt appreciation,
Joshua DuBoise

References

Balswick, J. O., and J. K. Balswick. 2014. *The Family: A Christian Perspective on the Contemporary Home.* Grand Rapids: Baker Academic.

Gottman, J., and J. DeClaire. 1998. *Raising an Emotionally Intelligent Child.* New York: Fireside/Simon and Schuster.

Gottman, J., and N. Silver. 1994. *Why Marriages Succeed or Fail and How You Can Make Yours Last.* New York: Fireside.

Gottman, J. M., and J. S. Gottman. 2007. *And Baby Makes Three: The Six-Step Plan for Preserving Marital Intimacy and Rekindling Romance After Baby Arrives.* New York: Crown.

———. 2017. *Avoid The Four Horsemen for Better Relationship.* Seattle: The Gottman Institute.

——— 2018. *The Science of Couples and Family Therapy: Behind the Scenes at the Love Lab.* New York: W. W. Norton & Company.

———. 2017. *Small Things Often: How to Build a Positive, Lasting Relationship.* Seattle: The Gottman Institute.

Glass, Shirley P. 1999. *Infidelity.* Washington, DC: Glass.

Glass, S. P., and J. C. Staeheli. 2003. *Not "Just Friends": Protect Your Relationship from Infidelity and Heal the Trauma of Betrayal.* New York: Free Press.

Jacobson, N. S., and A. S. Gurman. 2008. *Clinical Handbook of Couple Therapy.* New York: Guilford Press.

Johnson, S. M., and K. Sanderfer. 2016. *Created for Connection: The "Hold Me Tight" Guide for Christian Couples: Seven Conversations for a Lifetime of Love.* New York: Little, Brown and Company.

Köstenberger, A. J., and D. W. Jones. 2010. *God, Marriage, and Family: Rebuilding the Biblical Foundation.* Wheaton, IL: Crossway.

Niehuis, S., L. Skogrand, and T. L. Huston. *When Marriages Die: Premarital and Early Marriage Precursors to Divorce.* Retrieved May 30, 2017, https://ncsu.edu/ffci/publications/2006/v11-n1-2006-june/fa-1-marriages-die.php

Olson, D. H., J. D. DeFrain, and L. Skogrand. 2011. *Marriages and Families: Intimacy, Diversity, and Strengths.* New York, NY: McGraw-Hill Education.

———. 2014. *Marriages and Families: Intimacy, Diversity, and Strengths*, 8th ed. New York, NY: McGraw-Hill Education.

Warren, S. "Psychology of Attraction," July 25, 2018, Liberty University. EDCO806_LUO_8WK_MASTER_ImportedContent_20180504103646/EDCO806_Presentations/EDCO806_04_Psychology_of_Attraction (LMS)/res/index.html.

Williams, L., T. M. Edwards, J. Patterson, and L. Chamow. 2011. *Essential Assessment Skills for Couple and Family Therapists.* New York: The Guilford Press.